St. Patrick and Irish Christianity

Tom Corfe

Published in cooperation with Cambridge University Press
Lerner Publications Company, Minneapolis

Editors' Note: In preparing this edition of *The Cambridge Topic Books* for publication, the editors have made only a few minor changes in the original material. In some isolated cases, British spelling and usage were altered in order to avoid possible confusion for our readers. Whenever necessary, information was added to clarify references to people, places, and events in British history. An index was also provided in each volume.

LIBRARY OF CONGRESS CATALOGING IN PUBLICATION DATA

Corfe, Thomas Howell.
    St. Patrick and Irish Christianity.

    (A Cambridge Topic Book.)
    Includes index.
    SUMMARY: Relates what is known about the life and times of Saint Patrick, how he brought the Christian religion to Ireland, and the work of Christian missionaries in Britain and Europe.

    1. Patrick, Saint, 373?-463?—Juvenile literature. 2. Missions—Europe—Juvenile literature. [1. Patrick, Saint, 373?-463?. 2. Saints. 3. Missions—Europe] I. Title.

    BX4700.P3C63 1979   270.2'092'4 [B] [92]   78-56811
    ISBN 0-8225-1217-3

This edition first published 1979 by Lerner Publications Company
by permission of Cambridge University Press.

Original edition copyright © 1973 by Cambridge University Press
as part of *The Cambridge Introduction to the History of Mankind: Topic Book*.

International Standard Book Number: 0-8225-1217-3
Library of Congress Catalog Card Number: 78-56811

Manufactured in the United States of America.

This edition is available exclusively from:
Lerner Publications Company, 241 First Avenue North, Minneapolis, Minnesota 55401

Contents

This bell is reputed to be Saint Patrick's own, found in his tomb.

The elaborate shrine was made for it at Armagh about AD 1100.

PICTS

DALRIADA

STRATHCLYDE

?

Slemish Mt

Lough
Neagh

Strangford Lough

Whithorn

?

MAN

IRELAND

Irish Sea

Tara

Holyhead

Wicklow Mts

Caernarvon

Chester

BRITAIN

PEMBROKE

BRECON

Caerleon

Cardiff

?

Glastonbury

?

Tintagel

CORNWALL

**Irish raids on Roman Britain
about AD 400**

☐   Romano-British military bases

⬩   Regions with traces of Irish settlers

✚   Early monasteries

?   Possible sites of Patrick's birth

→   Irish raids

0   50 miles

0   80 km

1. How Patrick came to Ireland

In the days when the Roman hold on Britain was weakening and the Christian faith was taking root, Patrick was born at a small town somewhere in the west. We do not know just when he was born (perhaps about AD 390) and we do not know just where. The place was called *Bannavem Taburniae*, but it could have been near the Clyde, or on the Cumbrian coast, or in Wales, or near Glastonbury. Our information about Patrick, in fact, is very scanty, and so we have to make guesses at the truth. We are not even certain about his name; probably he only came to be called Patricius or Patrick late in life.

All that we can be fairly sure about is what Patrick tells us himself. Late in his life he wrote an account of how and why he had become a missionary; and his words, copied, re-copied and sometimes mis-copied by monastery scribes, have survived to our own day. His story is not very complete and not very clear.

Two hundred years after Patrick's death Irish churchmen began to write down what they could find out about his life and work. Naturally by that time memories had become a little vague and confused, and lots of strange, exciting stories were being told. Some of these seem to have been made up. People would be eager to believe that Patrick had visited *their* part of Ireland, been helped by *their* local king, converted *their* ancestors. Well-meaning preachers would embroider tales to impress their hearers about the miracles with which the holy Patrick had overcome his pagan enemies. Soon, for example, men were saying that there were no snakes in Ireland because Patrick had banished them.

But though we must be uncertain about many details of Patrick's life, archaeologists and historians can tell us something about the world in which he lived.

This statue of Saint Patrick was set up 1500 years after he landed. It is near Saul in County Down, where he is said to have founded his first church. On it is his name in the Irish language. The alphabet on page 36 will help you to read the letters.

The last days of Roman Britain

Patrick's father, he tells us, was called Calpornius, and he was a *decurion*. That means he was a wealthy and important official. Not only did he own a villa with an estate, slaves and servants, but he served as a member of the district council. He was one of those responsible for collecting the taxes and enforcing the laws throughout a region that was perhaps the size of a large modern county in England.

The power of the distant Roman governor in Londinium (London) was weakening. All too often his soldiers marched off to Gaul or Italy under an ambitious general who hoped to make himself emperor, and those left behind were occupied in the almost hopeless task of trying to ward off attacks from barbarian raiders, Saxons, Picts and Irish. More and more, decurions like Calpornius were left to act on their own. There was little help or advice now from London or Rome, and no troops to assist in local difficulties; simply orders to keep the district running as smoothly as possible and to collect more taxes for paying the soldiers. If, like Calpornius, the decurion owned a substantial estate, he probably had to meet the bulk of the local taxes out of his own wealth.

Patrick's grandfather was a Christian priest, and Calpornius himself was a deacon of the Church. Still, it was not a particularly religious home. Probably Calpornius only held his religious office because it meant his property was not so heavily taxed; moreover, it was sensible for a local official to be an active member of the state church. Throughout Roman Britain bishops and priests now worked alongside governors and decurions helping to enforce the authority of the empire, which had recently adopted Christianity.

Even though times were difficult and the future uncertain, Patrick's home life was comfortable enough. His education, however, was not very thorough. He never seems to have learned properly the official language, Latin, that his father and grandfather had to use so often; he was never very skilled at writing it. He spoke more easily the British of the country folk, a language like the Welsh still spoken today.

right: Coins issued by four generals who led revolts in Britain and tried to make themselves emperors.

General Carausius showed himself being welcomed by 'Britannia'.

General Allectus showed a ship of his fleet, which he hoped would keep Britain safe from attack.

Cardiff Castle. The rectangular outer wall is that of the Roman fort. Only the lower parts of these walls and towers were left before it was rebuilt about 100 years ago. As you can see, the Normans built a castle on a mound in the middle of the ruined Roman fort.

left: How a Christian of Roman Britain prayed. This is one of six figures, each about half life-size, painted on the wall of a chapel inside a villa at Lullingstone in Kent. Archaeologists have been able to put together the fragments of the wall-plaster.

General Magnus Maximus showed himself with a shield and a Christian standard.

The general who called himself 'Constantine III' showed himself with his foot on a defeated enemy.

Irish raiders

In those dying days of the great empire, raiders from beyond the seas frequently appeared off the British coasts. A hundred years before, forts had been built all along the Saxon Shore to provide some protection on the south and east, and there were similar defences in western Britain, where Patrick lived, to guard against the Irish. We know of a large new fort at Cardiff and a smaller one at Holyhead; even the great fort at Segontium (Caernarvon), built centuries before to subdue the Britons, had been re-occupied and reconstructed, to protect them this time. But even when these were linked with an early-warning system of naval patrols they were only partially successful. By the time Patrick was born Roman troops were in too much demand elsewhere for garrisons to be left in forts like Segontium and it had been abandoned. The Irish raiders came more frequently and in greater numbers, 'like dark swarms of worms which emerge from their holes in the heat of the noon-day sun', a miserable Briton wrote. Sometimes they even drove out the native Britons or settled alongside them in villages whose remains are still scattered over the

Remains of a stone 'Irishman's hut' on Holyhead Mountain in Anglesey. Most of these huts are between 17 and 22 ft (5 to 7 m) across.

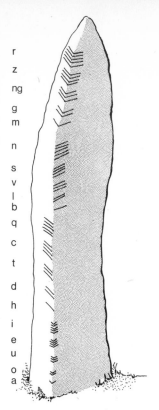

above right: Ogham letters used by the Irish for carving short inscriptions on the edges of wood or stone pillars. Usually words would be carved upwards from the bottom.

far right: This stone from South Wales has carved on it in Latin 'The Memorial of Voteporix the Protector'. Voteporix died about 540, and he was descended from an Irish chief who had settled with his people perhaps two centuries before. Carved on the edge of the stone is the Protector's name in oghams, in its Irish form, VOTECORIGAS.

left: We cannot be very certain of the appearance of the Irish warriors who captured Patrick, but they may have looked like this. On the following pages you can see something of what their weapons and boats were like.

hillsides in some parts of North Wales. In time Irish kings ruled in southern Wales and even in the mountains of Breconshire.

One day when he was sixteen a host of armed men descended on Patrick's home. Their leaders were tall fierce warriors with long hair gathered on top of their heads and braided, or streaming behind like horses' manes. Their cloaks and tunics were colourful, ornamented with brooches of gold, bronze and enamel. They carried iron swords and round wooden shields. Patrick's own ancestors would have looked much the same in the distant days before Rome and civilisation came to Britain.

These Irish raiders came in search of slaves, and with many others ('thousands' he tells us) Patrick was carried off. The unfortunate Britons were hustled into great boats made of greased ox-hides stretched over wooden frames, and there, crowded for some three days into a narrow space, frightened and seasick, they were carried to a land beyond civilisation.

left: The iron sword of an Irish warrior (22 in or 57 cm long), badly rusted away; but the decorated bronze scabbard found with it (17 in, 43 cm) remains almost perfect.

An Irish chieftain probably wore this hollow gold collar (or *torc*) about the time of the birth of Christ.

below: In the west of Ireland fishermen still use boats similar to, but smaller than, those that probably carried off Patrick. They are called currachs.

The drawing below shows a currach carved on the side of a stone cross in south-west Ireland about 1300 years ago.

Currachs were made by stretching and stitching ox-hides
over a frame of wood and basket-work.

11

ENGLISH	WELSH	IRISH	
One	ein	aon	The three languages (and
two	dau	do	most European languages)
three	tri	tri	have some words in common.
four	pedwar	ceathair	Here, as with many words, the
five	pump	cueg	Welsh use a 'p' where the Irish have a 'c' or a 'q'
Britain	Prydain	Cruithin	These words have the same
Britons	Prydyn	Cruithni	origin, though they do not now mean quite the same thing. The Greeks and Romans got their names for the island and people (Britannia, Britanni) from the native Britons' own words — the Welsh form. Later, the names Prydyn and Cruithni came to be applied only to the Picts who lived in Northern Britain.
son	ap	mac	Hewson, Pugh, MacHugh all mean 'son of Hugh'. Robinson, Probyn, MacCribbin are the same name.

You can see from comparing some words in the two languages why experts call Irish a Q-Celtic language and Welsh P-Celtic.

Pagan Ireland

In Ireland Patrick was for six years a slave, tending sheep, cattle and pigs for his master. In his loneliness he began praying many times a day to the Christian God whom in his youth he had neglected. Despite his humble position and dreary task he had plenty of time and opportunity to get to know his new masters, whose habits and way of life were so unlike his own.

Their language was not unlike his own British. Irish is also a *Celtic* language (it is still spoken in parts of western Ireland, though in much changed form), and the Irish, like the Britons, were a branch of the warrior race of Celts that had overrun western Europe in the centuries before the Romans came.

below left: The bank of a rath, about 130 ft (or 40 m) across, remains in a field, but there seems to be no trace of the buildings that once stood inside it. It is in Co. Louth.

below: The rounded hump of Slemish Mountain, where Patrick is said to have been a shepherd.

Untouched by the power and influence of Rome (though the Roman governor Agricola had once thought that he might conquer Ireland with a single legion), the Irish still kept to the warlike ways their British cousins had forgotten under Roman rule. They were a cattle-keeping people, for much of Ireland lacks the climate and soil to grow food crops of grain. It was a land of scattered farmsteads; there were no villages. Each family of farmers (and an Irish family usually included the cousins and their children) occupied a farmstead, a *rath*. Around it they cultivated a few fields of wheat or oats or beans if the soil were good enough, and they pastured their cattle. A rath consisted simply of a circular wall of earth or stone, broad but not very high, perhaps topped by a palisade of stakes. Inside were the round huts of wood and wattle (woven sticks) for the farmer's family, and room also to keep the stock at night, for the main object of the rampart was to stop the cattle from straying and protect them from wild beasts and casual thieves. The remains of these rath enclosures are still to be seen scattered over many parts of the Irish countryside, wherever they have not been destroyed by later plowing.

below left: In stony regions raths were stone-built, and there are much more substantial remains of these *cashels*. This model shows what a small cashel may have looked like when it was built.

below: Many raths had underground storage cellars, sometimes used for hiding in times of trouble. These are called *souterrains*. This one is at Drumena in County Down.

An Irish king and his people

Owes loyalty to Over King

Advice from druids and lawgivers

King

Services from nobles

Grants rath to farmer
Value: perhaps 24 cows

Stories, songs, information, skilled work from poets, bards, craftsmen

Gives services and pays annual rent
One year's rent, perhaps:
a fat cow
a salted pig
8 sacks malt
1 sack wheat
3 handfuls rush candles

Sometimes employs slaves

Kings, nobles and wise men

The cattle-farmers lived under the protection of warrior nobles, and they in turn owed service to the king. Ireland was a land of many kings, perhaps nearly two hundred of them, each at the head of his own people, his tribe or *tuath*. One of these kings, Miliucc, whose people lived north-east of Lough (lake) Neagh, was said to have been Patrick's master.

The king claimed descent from the tribal god. He was responsible for leading his people in wars and raids, and also for ensuring, through his magical powers and with the aid of his druids, that the sun and the soil brought good crops and healthy cattle. The king lived in a wooden hall set in a circular enclosure, a large rath that was distinguished by having one or two extra banks and ditches around it, built for him by his subjects. It seems likely that the royal hall was used for much communal feasting and the story-telling that always accompanied it, while about it the lean-to buildings set against the ramparts provided separate dwellings for the nobles and servants, for the youths sent to be reared as the king's foster-children, and for the king's advisers and entertainers. All these were ranked in order of wealth and importance. A noble's position depended on the number of farmers coming under his protection and owing service. His wealth would be counted in cattle and slaves, for the Irish had no money.

The professional men of the court were similarly ranked. The most important were the *druids*, learned and greatly respected advisers to the king in all matters, whether of government or religion. These scholar-priests spent their lives in finding out about the gods and their ways, and in passing on their knowledge to others. No one could write in ancient Ireland, so all knowledge had to be passed on by teaching and learned by heart. Next to the druids ranked the *law-givers*, whose duty it was to advise the king in matters of justice; they had to know, or pretend to know, of the judgments given by every Irish king in the past. Then there were *poets*, who were also seers; knowing the ancient tales of past heroes and kings, and knowing too the ways of nature, of stars, plants and animals, they could claim that their understanding allowed them to foretell the future. Lastly there were the *bards*, who memorised and recounted the tales of warriors and gods and added new stories of their own about them to entertain and instruct the king's guests.

The three banks and ditches of a royal rath can be picked out in this air photograph. You can also see traces of a circular house, a rectangular house, and a souterrain within it. Outside there seems to have been an oblong space with a bank and a fence round it, and perhaps ceremonies and games took place there. This is at Rathealy, Co. Kilkenny.

The hero-tales

The tales re-told so often among nobles and warriors and wise men of the king's court usually dealt with the deeds and adventures of long-dead heroes. A mighty warrior had only to be in his grave a few years and the bards throughout Ireland were competing with one another to tell more and more exciting stories of his exploits. Such a one was Cuchulainn, who must have lived (if he lived at all) some three or four hundred years before Patrick, and who won fame as the unconquerable defender of the northern kingdom of Ulster.

The mound of stones which can be seen from a great distance on top of Knocknarea in western Ireland is said to be Queen Maeve's tomb.

left: Cuchulainn, the great hero, eventually fell in battle. Mortally wounded, he tied himself to a stone pillar to die facing his enemies. The raven-goddess of death perched on his shoulder. This modern bronze statue is in the Post Office in Dublin, where in 1916 some rebels tried to set up an Irish Republic. They were defeated (and their leaders were executed) by troops of the British government. They looked back to legendary warriors like Cuchulainn for their inspiration, and the Irish Republic of today, which honours them as its founders, has set up this statue in their memory.

below: The huge stone mound uncovered by archaeologists within the sacred royal enclosure of Emain Macha.

The best loved of all the tales, one that was always being improved and added to, was called in Irish the *Táin Bó Cuailnge*, 'The Cattle-raid of Cooley'. It told how the armed hosts of Connacht, the western kingdom, had set out to capture the famous Brown Bull of Ulster, so mighty that fifty boys could play upon its back and a hundred warriors shelter in its shade. They were commanded by their Queen Maeve, so mysterious and powerful a being that even a thousand years later Shakespeare knew of her as Mab, Queen of the Fairies. She was eager to secure a bull even mightier than her husband's famous White-Horn. Led by their champions in their chariots, bearing javelins and thrusting-spears and iron swords, the army set off for the north.

The warriors of Ulster, all save Cuchulainn, could not come to meet them. Cursed by a mysterious sickness they lay asleep at Emain Macha, the royal rath of their High King. Cuchulainn, 'the Hound of Ulster', alone held off the enemy as the Connacht champions came forward one by one to fight and fall. The bards loved to add fresh stories, to linger over the de-tails of the insults that the champions hurled and the mighty blows they gave. In the end not even Cuchulainn could prevent the Connachtmen carrying off the Brown Bull and bearing it away beyond the Shannon; but the Bull of Ulster promptly fought the White-Horned Bull, tore it to pieces, and then rushed home to die, spreading a trail of destruction.

A bronze trumpet found near the foot of the hill on which Emain Macha stood, 6 ft 1 in (1.85 m) long. It was probably for royal ceremonies.

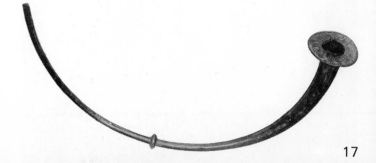

17

New Grange was erected by people who lived long before the Celts came to Ireland, and nearly 3000 years before Patrick. It is a huge burial mound. Inside is a passage lined with great stones, many with patterns picked out on them, and a burial chamber over 19 ft (6 m) high. The Celts thought of it as the home of fairy folk. Since these pictures were taken the Irish government has started rebuilding the mound to look as it did 4000 years ago.

Linked with the story of the *Táin* were many other tales, filling in the lives of the characters, explaining their motives, describing their adventures. There were a host of other stories, too, stories of the god-like races that had invaded Ireland at the beginning of the world, and memories of the Celts' own coming and of the peoples they had driven out or enslaved. These older peoples were remembered as giants and fairy folk, and said still to inhabit the great magical mounds they had built for their chieftains' bones. There were stories of adventurers and wanderers, men who had sailed to mysterious lands beyond the ocean. The western coasts of Ireland have hundreds of little islands stretching towards the setting sun, but beyond them lies a great open desert of water so that men wondered much what lay further to the west and out of sight.

Ireland in the time of St Patrick

ULSTER
Grianan
Slemish Mt
Lough Erne
Ben Bulben
Strangford Lough
Emain Macha
Armagh
Downpatrick
Knocknarea
COOLEY
CONNACHT
MEATH
Clew Bay
New Grange
Croagh Patrick
Slane
R. Boyne
Tara
R. Shannon
Aran Is.
Kildare
Wicklow Mts
LEINSTER
Mt Brandon
MUNSTER
Cashel

⊙ Royal raths of Kings or High Kings

0   50 miles
0   80 km

The High Kings of Tara

In Patrick's day the power of the Ulster kingdom, the home of Cuchulainn, had been shattered by a vigorous warrior king, Niall, who came from the west. Niall of the Nine Hostages he was called, and his power as overlord extended over most of the petty kings of central Ireland. He took hostages, their brothers or sons, from the rival kings of the north to dwell at his hall of Tara. He was a mighty war leader not only against the other kings of Ireland but in raiding across the Irish Sea, and it must have been one of the expeditions he sent out that had captured Patrick. His descendants, the *Uí Néill* (one branch later became the O Neills) were to reign long from the swelling green hill of Tara over the plain of Meath, the kingdom he had built up, and to claim the title of High King of All Ireland. But in the south west, at Cashel, a massive rocky stronghold, a rival dynasty of High Kings were overlords of Munster.

The trading ship that Patrick escaped in may have been carrying a cargo of Irish wolfhounds.

Patrick's escape

Somewhere in this land of warriors and herdsmen Patrick lived for six years. Then he made up his mind to escape and walked for many miles to a harbour far from his place of captivity. There he persuaded the crew of a trading ship to take him with them. It was an adventurous journey; the ship was driven ashore, apparently in some remote part of Britain, and after wandering, lost and hungry, for many days the sailors and Patrick were seized and imprisoned by his own countrymen. It was a long time before he eventually succeeded in making his way back to his own family at Bannavem.

On the low hill of Tara can be seen traces of many ancient buildings, including two royal raths linked together.

There had been changes. The links with Rome were near breaking point. Probably it was while Patrick was in captivity that the Imperial City had fallen to the Goths, and the Emperor Honorius had told the Britons they must now look after themselves. But even if there was no more help from Rome the British people went on thinking of themselves as Roman citizens, carrying on the government and traditions of Rome. Important local officials like the decurion Calpornius had even more to worry about now; in their moments of greatest difficulty they still sent hopefully to Rome for advice and assistance. Their colleagues in the Church, the bishops, still kept some links with the bishop of Rome, now generally known as the Pope.

Patrick entered the Church and became a priest. It was a very lively and energetic Church, but there were a good many arguments among British churchmen over matters of belief and worship.

Saint Germanus

In 429 the Pope sent a most important person to sort out the disagreements among the British bishops. His name was Germanus; he had been a soldier, a lawyer, and a governor of a province in Roman Gaul. Now he was bishop of Auxerre, a sincere and vigorous Christian. He travelled widely in Britain. He organised and inspired a British army to defeat an invading horde of Picts and Saxons; the Britons waited in ambush and then rose up with a great war-cry 'Alleluia!', making such an unearthly din that the invaders fled.

Bishop Germanus was concerned not only about the state of the Church in Britain but with the Christians of Ireland as well. It seems that there must, by this time, have been a good many Christians beyond the Irish sea, for apart from Christian slaves like Patrick there had been much trade between Ireland and Christian Europe. Merchants, like those who brought wine from southern Gaul, had sometimes settled and married; and there were, too, the Irish settlers in Wales and Scotland who had seen much of Christianity. But the Christian groups of Ireland were still few and scattered. They needed to be brought into touch with one another and organised under a bishop.

A bishop for the Irish

In 431 the Pope despatched a priest named Palladius to take charge of the Irish Christians. He worked, it seems, in eastern Ireland, around the Wicklow Mountains; it was near this stretch of coast that many of the Christians were to be found. Palladius' mission does not seem to have been very successful and probably he soon left Ireland.

About the same time the leaders of the British Church, having overcome most of their own difficulties, also took up the cause of the Irish Christians; and Patrick speedily came to their notice. As a returned captive and the son of a prominent citizen he must have had quite a reputation as an expert; they would naturally turn to him for information and advice about the country in which he had lived for so long.

Patrick was a modest man, dubious of his own fitness for the task. He did not look forward to leaving his family and friends. 'I am Patrick, a sinner, most unlearned, the least of all the faithful and utterly despised by many', he wrote. On the other hand he could never forget the people he had got to know so well twenty years before. Their need for someone to guide them along the path of Christianity was desperate. In his dreams he heard them asking him to 'come and walk amongst us once more'.

The bishops had some doubts about Patrick's fitness for the task, but in the end Patrick's sense of mission and the persuasions of his friends combined to send him back to the land of his captivity, dedicated as bishop to spending the rest of his days in winning the Irish to Christ.

2. How Patrick brought Christianity to Ireland

Probably it was in the year 432 that Patrick arrived back in Ireland. The tradition is that he landed in a part of the country not far from that he had known as a captive. The boat bearing the new bishop and his few helpers found its way through the narrow entrance of Strangford Lough, by way of shallow waters studded with islands and sandbanks, into the narrow estuary of the little River Quoile. A mile or so up the river was a large hill-fort, or *dun*, stronghold of the local king; in later years it was to become known as Dun-Patrick, or Downpatrick. The king was prepared to welcome Patrick and his mission; he even gave a large stone barn not far from the landing place to be used as a church, and here, at a place still called Saul ('barn' in Irish) Patrick began his work.

The ease with which Patrick found his way into this difficult harbour, the way in which the king welcomed him and accepted baptism seem to show that some sort of arrangement must have been made beforehand. Patrick in fact directed most of his appeals to the kings of Ireland; if they could be won over their people would speedily follow. He could offer them certain advantages. The Christian Church in the late Roman Empire had grown into a useful instrument of government, helping to make sure that the Emperor and his officials were properly respected. Irish kings may well have seen just how such an orderly, well-behaved Church could help them. Perhaps they were glad to challenge the arrogant claims of the druids, who thought themselves so wise and important and far-sighted, and demanded such a powerful position at court. Above all Patrick's simple faith in his God and his vivid preaching must have made a great impression. For one reason or another many Irish kings welcomed Patrick's teaching, and many of their kinsmen became priests themselves.

Of course Patrick often met difficulties and hostility. At one time, he tells us, he was made a prisoner and put in chains. But he was determined to carry out his task and in the end he set Christianity on a firm footing in the northern parts of Ireland.

These stone figures on islands in Lough Erne were probably carved when the first Christians mingled with heathens. One shows a two-headed pagan god and the other an abbot with crozier and bell.

The druids

The druids, with their massive learning and their strong position as advisers to the kings, were worried at this threat from over the sea. They warned people of the bishop's coming, sneering at the mitre and chasuble he wore and the crozier he carried:

> Adze-head will come,
> Hollow-head his mantle,
> Bent-head his staff,
> His table facing east,
> His people, chanting, answer
> Amen, Amen.

At Tara, so the story goes, the High King and his druids were holding a sacred spring feast. No fires save that at Tara itself might burn while the ceremony went on. Far away to the north, on the green hill of Slane beyond the Boyne River they saw points of light. It was Patrick lighting his own fires to celebrate Easter and challenge the druids, and one of them warned the king that if the hostile fire was not put out now, it would never die out in Ireland. (His fears were well-founded.) Patrick and the king's druids engaged in fierce argument, though the High King remained friendly to the old religion for many years after Patrick's death.

The legend of how Patrick lit his fires to defy the king's druids was always popular. This is how an 18th-century artist painted it on the ceiling of Saint Patrick's Hall in Dublin Castle.

22

The legends of Patrick

This is the part of Patrick's life of which we know least, and the part about which most of the far-fetched stories are told. The story of the Easter fires, for example, is not true, though it was written down by people who believed that it had happened, over two hundred years after Patrick's death. How far Patrick travelled from his northern base is not certain. He may have gone west into Connacht. He is said to have met the High King's daughters there and explained the idea of the Trinity, the three Gods in one, by using the little three-leaved shamrock. He is said to have climbed the tall conical mountain of Croagh Patrick, over-looking the rocky shores of the Atlantic and the many islands of Clew Bay. There he meditated for forty days, praying for the conversion of the Irish among stormy winds and torrential rain. (But perhaps whoever first told that story was thinking of Moses on Mount Sinai and adding a little Irish weather). Still, each year, thousands of pilgrims, often barefoot, climb the mountain in memory of his vigil. Perhaps he went as far as the southern kingdom of Munster and converted the High King there at his great rock of Cashel, which is now called Saint Patrick's Rock.

Modern pilgrims climbing Croagh Patrick.

left: The Rock of Cashel. The steep roofs and square tower of the church built by an Irish king early in the twelfth century can be seen, though it is over-shadowed by the ruins of the cathedral built along-side it later in the Middle Ages.

They will show you a rock there where Patrick sat (they will show you such rocks through the length and breadth of Ireland) and they will tell you a good story: of how during the ceremony of the High King's baptism the Bishop accidentally planted the pointed end of his staff upon the royal foot, piercing it to the ground. The King, who thought this very painful process was a necessary part of the baptism, made no complaint but bore it in silence to the end.

We can be sure that most of Patrick's activities took place in the north, at first around Saul and Downpatrick and later in the region of the former capital of Ulster, Emain Macha.

That famous sacred place of the days of Cuchulainn was no more than a massive mound now, set up over the burned remnant of the great building that had once stood there. On another hillside three miles away, called Ard Macha (the high place of the goddess Macha), the petty king Daire now held court, and Daire welcomed Patrick. Within the sacred circle of Daire's royal rath Patrick set up his church. It became the monastery and later the cathedral of Armagh. Soon it was claiming to be Saint Patrick's chief foundation, the head-quarters of Christianity in Ireland; and still today Armagh and its Archbishop hold the position in the Irish Church that Canterbury holds in England, that of supreme importance.

Each missionary saint like Patrick carried a pointed staff. In later days it was often treasured by his followers. Encased in bronze, it became the crozier that every abbot and bishop carried. This one, from County Antrim, is more like a walking stick, only just over three ft (98 cm) long.

below left: This ugly stone figure is still in the vestry of the cathedral at Armagh. She may represent the goddess Macha.

below: The present cathedral of Armagh stands on the hill. The curving street in this photograph follows the line of the royal rath, which became Patrick's monastery enclosure. From the earliest times important roads met at the rath.

24

How to convert pagans

On the whole Patrick seems to have found it fairly easy to bring the Irish to Christian beliefs. No Christians were martyred for their beliefs in Ireland, so there can have been few passionate or powerful defenders of the pagan ways. Partly his success was due to his appeal to the kings, to the fact that he was able to convince them that a Christian Church in their realms would bring with it some of the orderliness and efficiency that men still thought of as characteristic of the mighty Roman Empire. Partly it was due to his sincerity and faith and hard work. Partly, too, it was due to the way he treated the old beliefs of the Irish. The legends frequently tell of Patrick overthrowing heathen idols and setting up Christian churches on the spot. That means that often the country folk went on worshipping at the same spot as before, only in a somewhat different way. The great pillar-stones that the druids had set up to mark sacred places and graves now had crosses carved upon them. The wells and springs where farmers had prayed to a god or goddess to make sure their water supply was good now became holy wells where they prayed to a Christian saint instead. Sometimes the first churches were set in oak-tree groves, and oak-trees were sacred to the druids. In all this Patrick and those who followed him may have been challenging the power and beliefs of the druids but they were also making use of druid customs and druid holy places, making it easy for those who had trusted one religion to turn to another.

below: A richly carved stone at Turoe in County Galway, set up perhaps two or three hundred years before Patrick came to Ireland, and a pillar in County Armagh that was carved with crosses about 250 years after Patrick's time, though it may have been standing there long before.

below: Visitors to a holy well tie bits of rag or strings of beads to the trees about it. They hope that their prayers at the well will help cure ailments.

The story of Saint Bridget

The story of Saint Bridget shows what happened in one case. Saint Bridget, it is said, was born about twenty years after Patrick's death; but we know almost nothing about her life, nothing that we can be really sure about. What we do know is that the Celts of Britain and Ireland had long worshipped a powerful goddess who was usually called in Ireland Brigid. She was said to be daughter of the Dagda, chief of all the gods. Sometimes she was one, sometimes three sisters all with the same name, which simply means 'the exalted one'. Men invoked Brigid's help to protect their flocks and herds and bring increase, to inspire poetry and grant wisdom and skill in craftsmanship, to heal the sick and comfort the dying. She was all-powerful and ever-helpful. As the coldest weather of the winter began to depart and the sun seemed to be returning, men celebrated her festival joyfully.

Patrick and his followers could not deny that so useful and helpful a spirit existed. So she came to be identified with a Christian saint. Saint Bridget's festival is celebrated on the 1st of February, as Brigid's had been. The saint's shrine, with an ever-burning fire tended by virgins, was at Kildare, where formerly there had been a pagan sanctuary; the very name Kildare means 'the church of the oak-tree'. Saint Bridget's miracles took the place of the goddess's magic. Saint Bridget cared for the sick and poor, guided poets, wise men and craftsmen, protected the cattle and made the land productive; and she still does. Saint Bridget's crosses are still woven out of straw throughout Ireland and set up over the doorways of houses and barns to bring luck and safety. Saint Bridget is said to have made the first cross out of rushes to show a dying pagan king, but perhaps the cross is even older than that and represents the sun and its rays with which the goddess Brigid was linked.

Pictures and statues of Saint Bridget are common all over Ireland. This plaster figure stands guard over a holy well in County Clare.

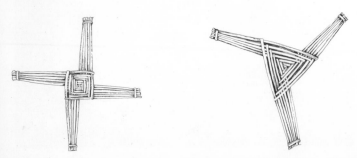

left: Some of the rush crosses woven in honour of Saint Bridget. These crosses are usually about 8 to 14 in (20 to 35 cm) across.

The results of Patrick's mission

Patrick is said to have died at Saul, where he had founded his first church and where he retired at the end of his life, perhaps in the year 461. Perhaps what he had succeeded in doing has been exaggerated because in later years his followers, and particularly the bishop of Armagh, wanted to show how much all Irish Christians owed to their great founder. But there can be no doubt that he drew together the scattered Christian groups that already existed and won over to the new Church many kings and their people. To a much divided country he brought a little of Rome's order and civilisation at the very time when they were being shattered in other lands, and he linked Ireland to the crumbling remains of the once-great empire. Perhaps, indeed, Patrick's mission should be seen as the last conquest of the Romans.

In the fifty years after Patrick's death Christianity spread throughout Ireland. The High Kings at Tara were unenthusiastic or even hostile, but the last pagan High King fell in a great battle on the slopes of Ben Bulben in 561. The druids and druidism disappeared, except so far as their beliefs and practices were taken into the new Christian faith. The other skilled and learned men carried on with their work, merely adding new, Christian, stories and laws and beliefs to their stock. Their new heroes were saintly missionaries, but their miracles were not unlike the heroic deeds of the warriors. Little groups of devout men and women, dedicated to the worship of the Christian God, grew up; often they lived near the royal rath and sometimes (as at Armagh) they took it over. These were the first Irish monasteries, and each was headed by an abbot, who might well be a prince of the royal family and would certainly be a close friend and adviser of the king. Often the abbot acted as bishop, ordering and leading the Christian churches throughout the kingdom.

below left: Ben Bulben with its sheer cliffs of limestone, is not far from Knocknarea, where Queen Maeve is said to lie. It is famous in the legends of Ireland as well as its history. In a churchyard at its foot is buried the best-known Irish poet, W. B. Yeats.

below: A king and an abbot setting up the corner post of a wooden church. This carving, dated about AD 900, is on a cross at the monastery of Clonmacnois. The king is bearded and carries a sword; the abbot wears linen tunic and mantle.

3. Irish monks and monasteries

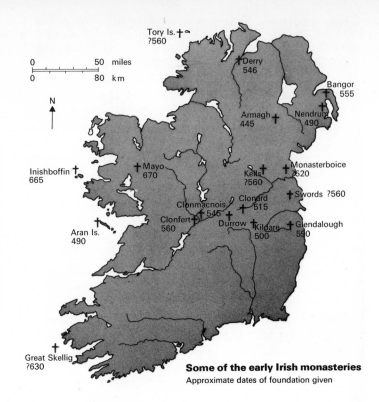

Some of the early Irish monasteries
Approximate dates of foundation given

About fifty years after Patrick's death a great change began in the religious life of Ireland. Its effects were as far-reaching as Patrick's own activities had been. From the eastern end of the Mediterranean Sea, from Syria and Palestine and Sinai and Egypt, from the very region where the Christian faith had been born, came new ideas of holiness and worship. Perhaps they were brought direct by missionaries, perhaps they came by way of Gaul and Spain. Irish churchmen heard how some very devout Christians had taken to leaving the cities and going into the desert, to lives of lonely prayer and thought, deliberately seeking extreme hardship. Instead of living close to the centres of wealth and power as the first Irish churchmen had, these hermits fled far from them. They rejected wealth. They did not want to enjoy comfort or be tempted by pleasant company, good food and conversation. They wanted to devote their whole lives to God.

The hermits took to dwelling together in single-minded, simple-living communities, monasteries. In Italy Saint Benedict took hold of the monastic idea and transformed it into a planned communal life where prayer, godly reading and hard labour were all laid down. A different version of the idea reached Britain and Ireland. We know little of the new monasteries in Britain; perhaps Tintagel in Cornwall became one about AD 470, and Glastonbury in Somerset soon afterwards. In Wales, in the sixth century, there were a number of Christian holy men (all in time were to be called saints) who settled in lonely places and gathered around them those who came to admire their example and listen to their teaching. In time the disciples became a monastic community, copying their founder in his way of life. In the far north, in what is now Scotland, Saint Ninian (who perhaps lived about the same time as Patrick) set up a monastery at Whithorn in Galloway and spread Christianity among the people of the region. He built himself a little stone church with plastered walls, the 'white house' or *Candida Casa*, which gave its name to his monastery.

The island monks

The same sort of thing happened in Ireland. Some devout Irishmen, accepting the eastern ideas of Christianity and holiness with enthusiasm, sought out the most desolate and remote places imaginable. Saint Enda is said to have been the first of these, and perhaps he picked up some of his ideas at Saint Ninian's monastery. About 490 the king of Munster granted him the Aran Islands, and on the biggest of these he set up his monastery.

The three Aran Islands are like broad shelves of rock rising nearly three hundred feet out of the Atlantic, almost barren and battered by waves. Life was hard there for the soil was thin and stony. It was only just possible to grow a few beans and pasture goats by adding layers of seaweed to the poor soil in the crevices and sheltered places of the rock. Here Enda and his 150 followers were certainly well away from any temptation to an easy life. Yet Aran was by no means out of the way.

On the lonely, rocky headland of Tintagel in Cornwall was a very early monastery, and the foundations of some of its buildings are beneath the narrow white rectangle (a medieval chapel) in the centre of this photograph.

below: Remains of the monastery huts perched on the ledge of the Great Skellig, with the mainland of Ireland beyond.

It was in full sight of land and easy to reach by boat. Fishermen and merchants passed close by every day. Enda's monastery attracted many young men seeking to copy his life of prayer and study. The islands became covered with little stone churches and the cells of the monks. Many who learned their faith under Enda in time moved on to found monastic settlements of their own.

Many other Irish monasteries were on islands, off the coast or in the many lakes of Ireland. The most lonely of all was on the Great Skellig, a spectacular pinnacle of rock off the farthest headland of south-west Ireland. The Skellig had no soil at all, and hardly any level rock. It was just possible to grow a few herbs in earth brought out from the mainland in baskets and planted in the sheltered crevices, and to keep a few goats. The monks lived a frugal life on fish and sea-birds and goats' milk. Their huts and tiny churches clung to the only sheltered ledge on the rock. Only when the sea was calm could they have any contact with the mainland, but that did not worry them. They had left behind for good what they thought of as the over-crowded world of greedy, selfish, irreligious men.

left: The original monastery of Clonard was within the rath now marked by a circle of trees, where the present church stands. All about it can be seen the traces of the 'University City.

right: At Clonmacnois are the grave-stones of many early monks. This one reads *OR DO THUATHAL SAER* (A prayer for Thuathal the craftsman).

Cities of learning and prayer

Other saintly Irishmen started their monasteries in more accessible spots. Saint Finnian's monastery at Clonard, in the heart of Ireland, was the first and greatest of these. Today the main road from Dublin to the west runs past its site, but there is hardly anything to be seen. Plunderers of many races, Viking, Norman, English and Irish have destroyed what was, in the sixth and seventh centuries, a great city of learning, a university.

Finnian, like most of the other leading abbots, came of a noble or royal family. He early visited Wales, and studied at the monasteries already established there, especially that of Saint David in western Pembrokeshire, where there were many Irish settlers. About 515 he set up his most important monastery by the banks of the Boyne, and soon young men flocked there to learn in far greater numbers than they had travelled to Aran. Finnian and others like him inherited and developed the traditions of learning and teaching that had grown up with the druids. It was said that there were 3000 students at Clonard, which would make it as large as many modern universities. Historians suspect that this figure must be exaggerated, yet those who have seen the fields around

Clonard from an airplane have been struck by the wide spread of disturbed ground in the neighbourhood of the monastery rath, with a host of mounds and hollows that seem to mark the place where once there stood hundreds of straw-and-wattle huts and workshops.

Many of those who studied under Finnian in the city of learning went on to found monasteries of their own, just as Enda's disciples from Aran had. Ciaran (or Kieran) went to the smooth green bank of the River Shannon at Clonmacnois, where the spreading ruins of his monastery can still be seen. Brendan came from the far southwest, where the tall mountain called Mount Brandon still has on its summit a little stone hut that is supposed to have been his hermitage. He visited not only Clonard but also many other monasteries along the western coastlands of Europe, in Brittany, Wales and Scotland, eager to find out the best way to live in holiness. In time he became known as Brendan the Voyager. Towards the end of his long life he settled at Clonfert, across the Shannon from Ciaran's monastery, to set up his own. Kevin, another young man of

royal descent, found his way over the desolate Wicklow Mountains to a secluded and beautiful valley called Glendalough where he settled as a hermit, until others sought him out to join him.

All these places grew and became famous because of the vigour and holiness of their founders, and many hundreds of students flocked to them. They were the first towns to appear in Ireland, towns dedicated to learning and to prayer.

Glendalough. Saint Kevin at first dwelt in a cave beside the further lake. When others came to join him, and later to live in the place that he had made holy, churches and a round tower were built further down the valley.

Life in the monasteries

The buildings of an Irish monastery were set within a rath or a *cashel* (the stone-walled kind of rath). There were churches, but even at a very large monastery like Clonard they would be small. This was partly because the Irish had not the skills or organisation to build a big church, but partly because they believed in solitary prayer rather than in frequent services for all the monks together, such as the Benedictine monks preferred. Most of the early churches were of oak-wood, with beams set to form a triangle at each end and the walls and roof of wattle-and-daub or thatch. Later the churches were rebuilt in stone, though for long these stone churches looked much as the wooden ones had. To make up for their small size there were many of them, at least seven in Saint Kevin's monastery at Glendalough, for example.

Around the churches were the huts of the monks, their cells. They too were of wattle-and-daub, except in the stony west; there were no wattles and no trees on Aran or the great Skellig, and at such places the monks' cells were of stone, built up to look like an old-fashioned beehive, each ring

above: The earliest monasteries in the more wooded parts of Ireland were built mostly of wattle and thatch and have left very few traces apart from stone crosses. This is how one might have looked.

above left: A monastery cashel on an island off the Kerry coast, with round and rectangular huts. Some of it has been washed away by the sea.

of stones set narrower until they closed together at the top. There was no mortar or cement, yet some of these strong little huts are still standing.

The bigger monasteries would have a guest-house for visitors and a refectory where the monks might eat. But their food was sparse and unattractive, for the monastery rules decreed enough to keep them alive but not enough to burden their stomachs or take their minds off their religious duties. That meant a diet of bread, beans and occasional other vegetables, supplemented from time to time by fish, apples and other wild fruit, milk, eggs, cheese, and, very rarely, meat.

above left: A stone church on Saint MacDara's Island off the coast of Connacht. It looks much like the older wooden churches, whose ends were formed of split tree-trunks held together at the top. You can see how the monks who built it fitted massive stones together, and built a steeply-sloping roof to keep off the Irish rain. The drawing shows how, when the artist of the Book of Kells wanted to show the Temple of Jerusalem, he drew it just like the steep-roofed little Irish churches of his day.

A beehive hut, called in Irish a *clochan*, of the Skellig monastery.

High crosses and round towers

The Celts had always set up tall stone pillars to mark sacred places or the burial spots of chiefs, and sometimes they had chiselled out intricate patterns on them. The monasteries took over this habit, sometimes re-using an old pagan stone and simply decorating it with a cross. In time their carving became more skilled and elaborate; working enthusiastically for their new faith the monks chiselled away, covering the stone surface with the symbols and the scenes from the Bible they knew so well. Every monastery had its tall cross, sometimes several of them. From the base of the cross the teacher spoke to his students or the priest preached a sermon to the laymen, and the stories they told were there for all to see, vividly carved and painted upon the stone. On the high crosses that still stand we can see Adam and Eve, Cain and Abel, Daniel in the Lions' Den, the birth of Christ and His arrest, a score of familiar scenes as the Irish monks of a thousand years ago imagined them. At the head of the cross the sculptors devised a means to support the overhanging arms, leaving a massive wheel of stone, the 'ring of glory', to act as stays. In the space at the cross head they carved on one side a great crucifixion scene and on the other the dreaded Last Judgement.

In later days another building was set up at many of the monasteries, a tall, slender round tower, often rising to a hundred feet or more and roofed with a conical cap. Its only door would be ten feet or more above the ground, and its only light came from four or five small windows. Probably these were built partly to house bells to summon folk to prayer, but principally as safe places of refuge when Viking raiders appeared on the scene.

left: The inscription on the base of this fine cross at Monasterboice, County Louth, tells us that it was set up by the Abbot Muiredach, who died in AD 922.

right: The arrest of Christ in the Garden of Gethsemane is shown on the lowest panel of Muiredach's Cross. Two very Irish-looking warriors have seized Him.

7th century

8th century

9th century

10th century

11th century

12th century

For centuries Irish crosses became more and more fully decorated, and told more stories; later they became simpler and showed just one or two figures.

Monks had to learn how to carve. These fragments of stone from the monastery of Nendrum show how they practised.

35

Books

Since learning mattered so much and since the Irish took such a passionate interest in the stories of the new religion, writing and books came to play a very important part in the life of the monasteries. Books were very few and very, very precious, but to have books at all meant that the monastery schools were immensely better equipped for teaching than the druids' schools that they had replaced. Patrick and his first followers brought with them the skill of writing, and soon the Irish monks developed a new style of lettering that was clear, easy to read and write, and very pleasant to look at, a style that is still sometimes used in writing the Irish language today. Every student learned to write and spent much of his time practising on waxed tablets with a stylus, copying out time and again the psalms. The earliest Irish book that still survives is a copy of the psalms that was probably made by Saint Columba about 560.

At that time the students were interested first and foremost in what the book had to say, and they wasted little time in decorating their pages. Before long they began to take more time and trouble over their work. It was exciting to be faced with a smooth, clean page of vellum, carefully prepared from the skin of a calf by a long and tedious process of stretching and scraping and soaking and rubbing over and over again with chalk and pumice-stone. The writers seized the opportunities given them by that beautiful surface. They drew and coloured pictures of the saints and scenes they wrote about, and they doodled colourfully around their text. Capital letters in particular began to snake out, winding and twisting in every direction. Strange birds and animals and fishes and funny little men appeared to fill in the gaps and peer round the letters. In the end whole pages were taken up with intricate interwoven patterns, whirling spirals such as the Celts had always loved to use on their gold and bronze ornaments, mingled with queer little twisted animal legs and heads, an idea picked up from the Anglo-Saxon peoples; the whole was rich with brilliant colour.

Such books took long years of work. When they were finished they were carefully guarded, both because of their beauty as works of art and because their contents were the sacred words of the gospels. They were kept in shrines of jewelled gold. Naturally, and tragically, most of them were lost forever in the days of the Viking raids, but a few, like the great Book of Kells displayed in the library of Trinity College, Dublin, can still be seen.

left: Part of a page from the oldest Irish book, perhaps in Saint Columba's own handwriting, and now kept at the Royal Irish Academy in Dublin.

The Irish alphabet.

right: A page from the most famous ancient Irish manuscript, the Book of Kells. You can read the Latin words and find the translation in Mark, ch. 15, verses 31-5. A warrior in jacket and pants squats at the foot of another page *(far right)*.

inludentes adalter uicinum cumscr
bis dicebant alios saluos fectt se
ipsum nonpotest saluam facere
xps resisrahel discendat nunc
decruce utuideamus & credamus
Qui autem cruciffixi erant
con unciebant eum
Facta hora sexta tenebre
facttesunt super totam
terram usque adhoram nonam
& hora nona exclamauit
ihs uoce magna dicens is
hello hello lamasa becthani quod
est interpractatum dsds meus ut
guid me direliquisti & quidam
decircumstantabus audientes dice
bant ecce heliam uocat iste

4. Missionary monks in Britain and Europe

The Irish monks mixed enthusiasm for spreading the word of God with their desire for an austere and lonely life. Having discovered this wonderful new truth they could not resist the urge to spread it, at whatever cost. Some of the most energetic of the saints started not one monastery but several. We can picture them striding along the trackways that criss-crossed Ireland in search of a friendly king with some remote island, a cave, or a spare rath that he was willing to grant the man of God. Within the monastery there was silence, and unnecessary gossip was punished with a beating; 'Pray daily, fast daily, study daily, work daily' was the rule. Outside the monk would be only too ready to broadcast his learning, to win over doubters, to join in arguments. In coarse garments, a white linen tunic covered by a drab, brown woollen cape with a cowl over his head and sandalled feet, he carried a staff, a heavy leather bag over his shoulder with his precious books, and a small bell of iron or bronze to summon his listeners. He had cut himself off from home and friends to seek God in his own hard way and to help others along the same difficult path.

The search for true holiness

Like the hermits of Sinai and Syria and Egypt, Irish monks found some peculiar ways to holiness. They believed that suffering pain helped them to concentrate on truly godly thoughts. According to the admiring monks who, long afterwards, wrote and perhaps embroidered the life-stories of these exceedingly holy men, some chose to stand daily in icy rivers to say their prayers; some deliberately set out to infect themselves with loathsome diseases; some fasted, others knelt or prostrated themselves hundreds of times a day; one vowed never to indulge in the pleasure of scratching himself.

But most were more sensible. It was hardship enough to leave family and friends for ever. If you could leave your fellow-countrymen as well, venture out on the great wastes of the sea in a tiny, tossing currach, visit strangers with foreign tongues and outlandish, pagan customs, then this was true holiness. In the century after the principal monasteries were founded many earnest Irishmen set out to seek exile for Christ.

The voyagers

In some ways the missionary saints were carrying on an Irish tradition that had started long before Patrick. Irish boats were small (usually only just big enough to carry the twelve companions that a missionary liked to take with him) but they rode easily over the Atlantic waves, and Irishmen from earliest times had made their way to the lonely islands off their western coast. They had voyaged up and down the western coasts of Europe, too, settling in Scotland, Wales and Brittany. They remembered tales of gods and heroes who had ventured out to sea, of King Bran who had set off with three currachs to search for a land of pleasure, food and beautiful women, and of Mael Dúin, whose voyage took him to no less than thirty islands in the western ocean, each with its own magical wonders and strange delights.

With this tradition of voyaging behind them and a passion to spread word of their faith the Irish monks set out. Saint Brendan 'the Voyager' certainly travelled widely among the Celtic peoples of the European coastlands, and later story-tellers credited him with having carried out a wonderful voyage far into the Atlantic to discover the earthly paradise. Until quite recent times map-makers marked Saint Brendan's Isle far out in the open ocean.

A modern drawing of the lands said to have been visited by Saint Brendan on his legendary voyage.

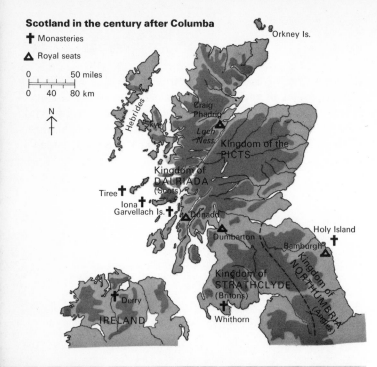

Scotland in the century after Columba

✝ Monasteries

△ Royal seats

0 — 50 miles
0 — 40 — 80 km

N

Orkney Is.

Hebrides

Skye

Craig Phadrig

Loch Ness

Kingdom of the PICTS

Kingdom of DALRIADA (Scots)

Tiree ✝

Iona ✝
Garvellach Is. ✝

Dunadd △

Dumbarton △

Holy Island

Bamburgh △ ✝

Kingdom of STRATHCLYDE (Britons)

Kingdom of NORTHUMBRIA (Angles)

Derry ✝

IRELAND

Whithorn ✝

Saint Columba

The most important of the missionary saints, and one whose voyage certainly did take place, was Columba.

Columba was born about 521 in Donegal. He was a direct descendant of King Niall, and a cousin of the king who now ruled over north-west Ireland. Like many young noblemen he determined to be a priest, and he studied at several of the monastic schools, including Clonard. He learned also the older skills of poetry, studying at a bardic school, and in later life he helped to defend the poets when other churchmen and kings sought to do away with these relics of the Irish past. His first monastery was set up near his cousin's court at the great stone hill-fort of Grianan. It was in an oakwood by the river, and it is still called Derry (oakwood) or Londonderry, though no trace of the monastery remains in the present city.

In the following years Columba travelled throughout Ireland, vigorously brushing aside difficulties to set up a number of other monasteries. There was Durrow (another oakwood) and perhaps Kells and Swords (these three are all in the rich plain of Meath), and lonely Tory Island off the Donegal coast. We know that Columba was very active, but we cannot be sure whether he or some of his followers at a later date actually established these monasteries.

About 560 Columba apparently quarrelled with another abbot. The story goes that it was over a book — the very one that still exists in Dublin. Columba is said to have copied it from one belonging to his fellow abbot without bothering to ask permission. The other claimed that the copy belonged by right to him, and the High King of Tara supported this rather selfish attitude. Columba in fury roused the UiNeill and their friends, and a great battle on the slopes of Ben Bulben took place during which the High King was killed. It seems likely that much more than a quarrel over a book was at the root of the trouble, for the High King was the last great enemy of the Christian monks in Ireland and with his death the Church finally triumphed. From 561 onwards the monasteries dominated Irish life.

left: From inside the ramparts of the Grianan, Columba's royal cousins could survey much of the Ulster they ruled.

The mission to Scotland

Whether because he was ashamed of his part in the quarrel or simply because his missionary zeal carried him overseas, Columba set off in 563 for Scotland. Here, on the west coast, in the region now called Argyll, the Irish rovers had built up a kingdom called Dalriada. The very name 'Scotland' in fact comes from these settlers, for in Roman days the 'Scots' were dwellers in Ireland. The seas are narrow between Scotland and Ulster, and passage is easy between the two lands. So Columba set off to join his fellow countrymen, who were still warring with the older inhabitants, the Picts.

Columba established a famous monastery on the little island of Iona, where not long ago archaeologists found traces of what may have been Columba's own stone cell. Most of the first monastery buildings were of the usual wood and wattle, and there was an encircling wall and ditch. Like so many of the monasteries back in Ireland, Iona very soon attracted students and became a great centre of learning.

It was also a base for much missionary activity. Columba himself travelled far afield, throughout the Scots settlements and beyond into Pictland. As an Irish prince he had great influence; and though he seems to have been generous and humane he was also a very forceful person. He sent out disciples who were drawn as if by magnets to the many islands off western Scotland, to Tiree and Skye and the tiny Garvellach Islands, and on to the farther Hebrides and the Orkneys, even into the Arctic seas, where in time Irish monks settled in the Faroes and Iceland.

Columba himself set off along the Great Glen to meet the hostile king of the Picts. On the way he encountered the Loch Ness monster, which unwisely attempted to swallow one of his followers. Columba spoke to the beast so forcefully that it seems to have been hiding ever since. Naturally, when he arrived at the Pictish king's stronghold he found little difficulty in bursting open the closed doors and persuading him to accept Christian missionaries in his kingdom.

So widely respected was Columba that when the king of Dalriada died the Scots turned to Columba for advice on whom should succeed. Aidan, the prince chosen by Columba, was duly enthroned and blessed by the abbot; he was an active ruler, and as his power spread so Columba's disciples wandered farther afield. In time Aidan's descendant, Kenneth Mac-

This is how the monk who wrote Columba's life-story and a Scottish painter of a hundred years ago imagined Columba preaching before the King of the Picts.

Alpin, united Picts and Scots; from Kenneth, and from Columba's chosen King Aidan, Queen Elizabeth II of England is descended.

In time Celtic churches, high crosses and monastery walls spread over the western parts of Scotland. In the Pictish lands Christianity took hold more slowly, and though Columba's followers must have founded many small monasteries there we know little of them. In time the Christian cross began to appear on the stone monuments of the Picts, and little stone churches, even round towers like the Irish ones, spread through eastern Scotland.

A carved stone of about the eighth century from the Shetland Isles shows four priests wearing hooded cloaks, some carrying book satchels.

A modern statue of St Aidan stands on windswept Holy Island.

The mission to Northumbria

The influence of Iona continued to spread long after Columba's death in 597. In the next century missionaries from Iona reached Northumbria, now once again a heathen land under the Anglo-Saxon invaders. There they founded their own island monastery on Lindisfarne, Holy Island. Aidan, a monk from Iona, became both its abbot and the bishop of the Northumbrians. As a Briton had, 200 years before, carried Christianity to the Irish, so now the Irishman Aidan brought Christianity back to Anglo-Saxon Northumbria.

Lindisfarne flourished as its monks gained a reputation for goodness and simplicity. The historian-monk Bede, who lived soon after and not far away, described it: 'There were very few houses besides the church, no more than were barely sufficient for their daily living. They had also no money, but cattle; for if they received any money from rich folk they gave it at once to the poor. The whole concern of these teachers was to serve God, not the world, to feed the soul, not the belly.'

It was like many another Irish monastery.

The Celtic Church and the Roman Church

The Irish monks and those they converted faced a difficulty. Some of the customs they brought with them differed from those of the missionaries from Rome who had converted the other Anglo-Saxon kingdoms. The Irish celebrated Easter at a different date; their Christianity was built up around the monasteries and their active, all-powerful abbots, where the Romans saw their bishops as key men, responsible for setting up churches and for the guidance of all Christians; and the Irish shaved their heads in a distinctive way, across the front from ear to ear instead of on the crown of the head. (Perhaps it was a way they had inherited from the druids.)

These things did not matter in themselves, but they caused awkward disagreements. The churchmen on each side insisted that they, and they alone, understood God's wishes in these matters, and got extremely heated in their arguments. It was left to the king of Northumbria to judge between them at a meeting in the monastery of Whitby in 663. Colman, who had come from Iona to follow Aidan as abbot and bishop, was the loser. Anglo-Saxon England had rejected the Celtic fashions

above: This grave-stone on Holy Island seems to show the Vikings who raided this monastery (and so many others) in the eighth and ninth centuries.

left: The Lindisfarne copy of the Gospels was written on Holy Island about 700. Some of its pages are very similar to those in the Book of Kells, but this is rather different; it is a picture of Saint Mark, and shows how the monks worked at copying their books.

of Christian worship, just as it had, a century or two before, defeated the Celts themselves and driven them out. But many of the traditions of the Irish Church lingered on in northern England. Not long after Colman's departure the monks of Lindisfarne began copying a magnificent version of the gospels, just like the beautiful books of Ireland; and many of the Northumbrian churches set up their own high crosses.

As for Colman, he set off with his Irish monks and many English followers to return sadly to Iona. Then he went back to Ireland and found a little island for himself off the wild coast of Connacht. Even there troubles followed, for the Irish and the English among his monks disagreed and he had to found a separate monastery for the Northumbrians inland at Mayo.

right: Saint Matthew as the artist of the Book of Durrow, a seventh-century copy of the Gospels, drew him. His hair seems to be cut back in the special form of tonsure (haircut) used by Irish monks. But as you can see from the painting on page 41 some people think the Irish tonsure was just across the top of the head, leaving a fringe in front.

43

Saint Columban

Saint Columban, who was born about twenty years after Columba, travelled even further afield. He does not seem to have started on his wanderings until quite late in life, perhaps when he was nearly fifty. He had spent many peaceful, studious years at the monastery school of Bangor, in Ulster. Then he decided to set off for Europe with twelve companions.

They went by way of Britain and Brittany into the domains of the Franks. The Franks had ruled in Gaul for more than a hundred years and had long been Christians, at least in name. But theirs was a troubled country where brothers and cousins warred and murdered for the thrones of three separate kingdoms, and the Church had little effect on the way people lived. Murder, magic, paganism, sin of every description shocked the Irish visitors.

Columban's party made its way to the court of the king of the East Franks. They were welcomed and allowed to settle in the ruins of an old Roman fort in the Vosges Mountains. They faced hardship and food shortage at first, and some hostility from the neighbours; but their single-minded devotion, their skill and learning and generosity soon attracted local people to join them. It became necessary to set up two more monasteries nearby, one of which became in time the great abbey of Luxeuil.

A Frankish warrior on horseback, from a grave-stone of about AD 700 in northern Germany.

Travels of St Columban
in the lands of the Franks and Lombards

NORTHUMBRIA
Bangor
0 50 miles
0 80 km
R. Elbe
MERCIA
Burgh Castle
N
WESSEX
KENT
R. Rhine
Aachen
Kingdoms of
the FRANKS
Wurzburg
R. Seine
Luxeuil
R. Loire
St Gall
R. Rhone
LOMBARDY
Bobbio
† Monasteries

44

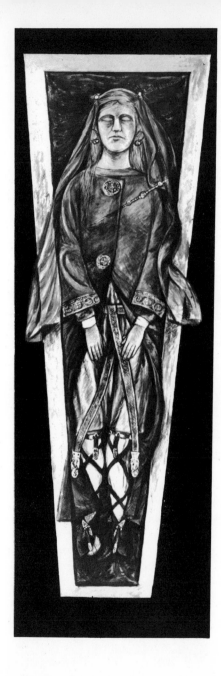

left: Though the Franks were supposed to be Christians they were a warlike, barbaric people. They carried on many pagan customs like burying some of their belongings with the dead. This picture shows a Frankish queen, whose tomb was found near Paris, as she would have looked when she was first buried about AD 750.

right: Some of the glassware, brooches, beads and pottery found in Frankish graves.

The Rule of Saint Columban

Columban drafted a set of rules for his new followers, probably very similar to the ones he would have obeyed himself at Bangor. These rules still survive. They start by reminding us: 'First of all we are taught to love God with the whole heart and the whole mind and all our strength, and our neighbour as ourselves'.

Then they lay down the monk's duties: to obey his seniors and be ever humble, to keep silence or speak only with care and caution, to eat and drink sparingly, to think only noble thoughts and to sing psalms or say prayers many times a day.

They list the penalties for misbehaving, even in very minor matters. Not waiting for grace at table, failing to say 'Amen', smiling at prayers (or worse, laughing out loud), telling idle tales. This kind of offence and many equally trivial could earn an absent-minded brother from six to fifty strokes with a strap on his hand, a severe fast, or the imposition of complete silence.

These rules of Columban seem petty and harsh. They were meant to help men who wanted to live in a truly saintly way amidst the temptations of a difficult, troubled world. The people of Gaul found them admirable and inspiring, and they were widely copied in Frankish monasteries. Not until the time of the Emperor Charlemagne, two hundred years later, were they replaced by the Rule of Saint Benedict.

About 200 years after the death of Saint Gall the monks who had settled at his hermitage planned a spacious new monastery for themselves. This is a simplified copy of the plan they used, and the drawing opposite shows what their new monastery would have looked like.

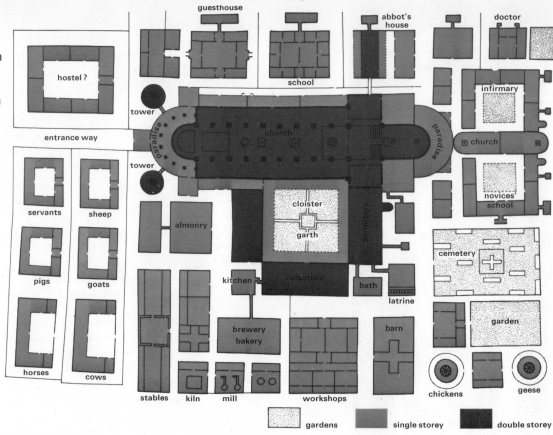

gardens | single storey | double storey

The travels of Columban

Like a good many successful missionaries, Columban was not very good at seeing other people's points of view. In time he quarrelled both with the local Frankish bishops over small matters and with the evil-living Frankish king over more serious ones. He and his Irish followers were ordered out, though his Frankish followers were allowed to continue his work in the monasteries he had founded. The unwanted Irishmen made their way back to the sea-coast but bad weather prevented them from sailing for home and eventually they resolved to set off for the city of Rome itself. Columban had, for many years, been exchanging letters with the Pope, full of good advice on both sides.

They went by a roundabout route, taking boats along the great rivers of France and Germany. They travelled into the wild, mountainous country that is now Switzerland, and there, at the farthest reaches of the Frankish Kingdom, they found themselves among pagans with true missionary work to do. One of Columban's followers, Gall, stayed behind as a solitary hermit; later a famous monastery was to be founded at the hermitage and bear his name.

The rest of the party climbed on over the Alps into Italy. There at last Columban settled to found the most famous of his monasteries at the end of his long life. It was at Bobbio, high in a pass of the Apennine Mountains. Columban died in 615 but his monastery, drawing monks from all over Europe and training them in the Irish traditions of scholarship, remained for long the most renowned in northern Italy. Its monks built up one of the finest libraries in all Christendom, copying out all the available works of learning and religion.

below: Fursa used Burgh Castle, a former Roman fort, as Columban used Annegray and Patrick used the dun of Armagh, to shelter his monastery.

Missionary saints and scholars

Columban was by no means the only Irish monk to exile himself in Europe. He was not even the first. Thirty or forty years before Fursa had gone to Gaul after first trying to establish himself on the coast of East Anglia. The monastery he had founded in an old Roman Saxon Shore fort granted him by the East Anglian king had been threatened by the pagan King Penda of Mercia, so he had crossed the narrow seas to Gaul. There he, and later his two brothers, had founded several monasteries.

In the centuries after Fursa and Columba many other Irish missionaries set off in their footsteps, spreading their godly enthusiasm through the length of civilised Europe. Some went beyond, into the lands of the pagans in central Germany. Saint Kilian and his companions sailed up the River Rhine and

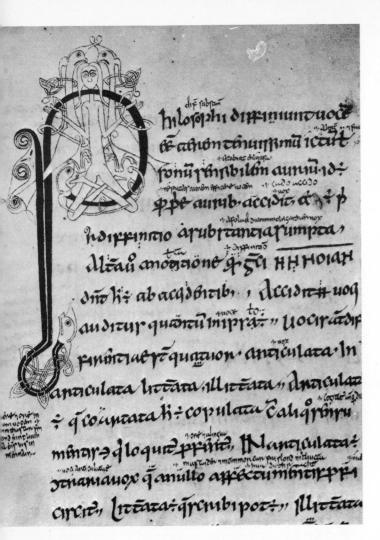

A page from a textbook of Latin copied by an Irish monk at St Gall about 850. Notes have been added between the lines and in the margins in the Irish language.

then made their way eastwards into unknown lands, spreading the gospel among chieftains and villagers until they were murdered at Wurzburg. Many others stayed in the lands of the Franks; even though they were foreigners with strange ways and an outlandish tongue some earned so much respect that they were made bishops, to direct and organise all the Christian life about them. More often they founded their own monastic settlements, as Columban had, setting an example of good works and learning for all the folk around. Moreover, many Frankish noblemen, inspired by the Irish example, themselves organised monasteries after the Irish pattern.

Yet other Irish wanderers earned reputations as scholars, either within the walls of their monasteries or at the courts of the Frankish kings. When in time the Emperor Charlemagne determined to restore and revive learning throughout his empire, and sought out the best scholars of Christendom, many of those he chose to advise him and teach in his schools were Irish. Irish monks wrote poems in praise of Charlemagne's victories, textbooks of Latin grammar, learned volumes on the sun and the stars. Dicuil, an Irishman at the court of Charlemagne's successor at Aachen, became the most famous geographer of his age. He could write of the farthest bounds of the world for he learned from Irish monks of the lands in the far north, of Iceland (which he called Thule) where the summer sun never truly set, so that even at night 'one can do whatever one wishes, even pick the lice from one's shirt.'

The vigour of Irish missionaries and bishops, the skill of Irish craftsmen in lettering and stonework, the scientific and religious learning of Irish scholars, even perhaps Irish music and poetry, all these were admired throughout Europe. Copied and adapted and developed, spreading from monasteries and schools and bishops' cathedrals, Irish ideas and ways became a part of the European way of life. They played an important part in laying the foundations for the new civilisation that was growing up in Europe as it left behind the 'Dark Ages' of upheaval. The medieval world, with its fine churches and universities, its literature, learning and arts, owed much to the wandering Irish monks and the ideas they carried with them.

Index

Acknowledgments

Illustrations in this volume are reproduced by kind permission of the following:

front cover, pp. 10 (currach), 16 (Knocknarea and statue), 19 (Tara), 23, 27 (Ben Bulben), 31 Bord Failte Eireann; pp. 3, 10 (torc), 17 (trumpet) National Museum of Ireland; pp. 5, 22 (Janus figure) Northern Ireland Tourist Board; pp. 6–7 (coins), 43 (Lindisfarne Gospels), 45 (grave goods) British Museum; pp. 6, 9 (hut circle), 43, 47 (Burgh Castle) Department of the Environment; pp. 7, 12 (Slemish Mt), 24 (Armagh) Aerofilms Ltd; pp. 9, 22, 45 (reconstruction) Thames & Hudson Ltd; pp. 10 (sword and scabbard), 13 (souterrain), 24 (crozier), 25 (Kilnasaggart cross) Ulster Museum; pp. 12 (rath), 15, 29 (Tintagel), 30 (Clonard), 32, Cambridge University Department of Aerial Photography; p. 13 (model) Cork City Museum, photo Prof. M.H.O'Kelly; p. 16 (Emain Macha), 35 (Nendrum fragments) Ancient Monuments Branch, Ministry of Finance Northern Ireland; pp. 18, 22 (painting), 25 (Turoe stone), 27 (Clonmacnois panel), 29 (Skellig), 30 (grave slab), 33 (St MacDara and clochan), 34, 35 (arrest of Christ), Commissioners of Public Works in Ireland; pp. 24 (Macha), 25 (holy well), 26, 40, Edwin Smith; p. 33 (drawing of church) from L. de Paor *Early Christian Ireland* (Thames & Hudson Ltd); p. 35 (crosses), Ruth Brandt, from *A Guide to the National Monuments of Ireland* by Peter Harbison, Gill & Macmillan Ltd; p. 36, Royal Irish Academy, photo Green Studios; p. 37 and back cover Trinity College Dublin, photo Green Studios; p. 39, Geoffrey Ashe; p. 41, detail of a painting by William Hole in the Scottish National Portrait Gallery; p. 42 (Aidan) Northumbria Tourist Association, photo Charles Spencer; p. 42, National Museum of Antiquities Scotland; p. 44, Landesmuseum für Vorgeschichte, Halle; p. 47, Alan Sorrell and Thames & Hudson; p. 48, Stiftsbibliothek, St Gall. The poem on p. 22 is from L. Bieler, *Ireland: Harbinger of the Middle Ages* (Oxford University Press). The Department of the Environment photographs are Crown copyright, reproduced with the permission of the Controller of Her Majesty's Stationery Office.

front cover: The top part of the stone cross of the Abbot Muiredach, from the monastery of Monasterboice in County Louth (see page 34). The very top of the cross is made in the shape of a little church of wood or stone. Then there is a scene from the Old Testament, showing Moses on the mountain, supported by Aaron and Hur and watching the struggle of Jews and Amalekites. Below this is the Crucifixion; the man on Christ's left strikes him with a spear, while he on the right offers a drink from a cup. Two angels are supporting Christ's head. The figures to the far left and right may be soldiers on guard and disciples at prayer. In the panel below the cross-head Christ is risen and enthroned, offering a book to St Paul on his left and a sceptre to St Peter on his right. Probably these scenes were once brightly painted and used to help in teaching the Bible story.

back cover: A page from the Book of Kells. The artist has enjoyed decorating it so much that you will find it very difficult to read the Latin words, but perhaps you can pick out the big I and P of the words *In Principio*, the opening of St John's Gospel. If you look closely you will find a harpist, a man drinking, another with a book, and lots of strange birds and animals.

Drawings by Anna Mieke
Maps by Visual Art Productions, Oxford

The Cambridge History Library

The Cambridge Introduction to History
Written by Trevor Cairns

The Cambridge Topic Books
General Editor Trevor Cairns

The Cambridge History Library will be expanded in the future to include additional volumes. Lerner Publications Company is pleased to participate in making this excellent series of books available to a wide audience of readers.

Lerner Publications Company
241 First Avenue North, Minneapolis, Minnesota 55401